D1058753

Lonely Planet

50 Festivals

TO BLOW YOUR MIND

Contents

Just one big party

Music

Off the wall

Introduction

There's something about festivals, be it a giant, joyous party or a respectful honouring of tradition; a seemingly bizarre adherence to ritual or a celebration of a quirky obsession; it's a uniquely human thing to be involved in. We like to get together to dance, sing, eat, laugh, drink, dress up, light fires, take our clothes off, throw tomatoes at each other, roll around in mud – just about anything really, but we seem to like doing it in really large groups with bags and bags of enthusiasm.

Why is it that we behave in this way? Because we're pleasure seekers? Because we're obsessives? We think it's because festivals are a life-affirming example of the inherent goodness in humanity. They take our desire to have a good time with our friends to a global level.

They kick-start because of our passions and our wish to spread and share our joy with as many other people as possible. But they continue and thrive because they ignite curiosity and go on to promote understanding, compassion and a greater acceptance of the human race, and all the crazy fun and fervour that comes with it.

All action

WWW.BALLOONFIESTA.COM;
FIRST WEEK OF OCTOBER.

Albuquerque International Balloon Fiesta, Albuquerque, USA

WHAT ARE WE TALKING HERE? PARTY BALLOONS?

If you go in expecting something like that, then you are going to be totally blown away (pun intended). This annual fiesta in New Mexico is the largest hot-air balloon festival in the world, with more than 500 of these spectacular aircrafts taking to the skies for nine days each October.

THE SKY LOOKS MAGICAL.

The sight of enormous balloons floating serenely through the New Mexico skies in all their kaleidoscopic colour is breathtaking. Keep your eyes peeled for the quirky and unusually shaped balloons – there's nothing quite like seeing a skyscraper-sized turtle floating overhead.

CAN WE JUMP ON BOARD AND GET A VIEW FROM UP HIGH?

While the festival is flooded with hardcore enthusiasts and serious professional balloonists who compete in races and other exhibition events, it's also open to curious onlookers. It's possible to walk around the field while the balloons are being lit and inflated, and book a ride on one also. Get in early though, as rides in the balloons sell out fast.

Argungu Fishing Festival, Kebbi, Nigeria

WE'RE A BIT SCEPTICAL AS TO HOW EXCITING FISHING CAN BE.
Well, let these West African fishermen show you a thing or two.

WHERE ARE THE RODS?
Exactly. This is where it gets interesting. The festival centres around a competition where approximately 35,000 fishermen wade into the water with hand nets and try to outdo each other by grabbing the biggest fish they can see. Fishermen can work in pairs, but they must catch their fish by hand. There was once a winner who dragged an 80-kilo catfish ashore. Not as boring as you first thought, right?

NO, THIS IS NOT WHAT WE EXPECTED.
The whole thing started over 80 years ago as a peace-making exercise between the Argungu people and their neighbours from Sokoto. It has grown to be one of the most popular festivals in West Africa, drawing in massive numbers for the fun and the spectacle. Oh, and it might also have something to do with the prizes. The lucky winner takes home around US$8000 and a new minibus. Not bad for a day's work.

WWW.HOLIFESTIVAL.ORG;

END OF FEBRUARY OR EARLY MARCH.

Holi, India and Nepal

CAN'T YOU NARROW DOWN THE LOCATION FOR US A BIT MORE?

Holi, or the Festival of Colour, as it has come to be known, is primarily a Hindu festival and it's celebrated with wild parties and crazy colour fights all over India and Nepal in areas with large Hindu populations. You'll know you've found one when you spot the revellers who look like they've walked through a rainbow waterfall.

A COLOUR FIGHT?

Holi is a celebration of the victory of one's inner good over evil but has basically become a frolicking free-for-all involving coloured powder and water. In a joyous and raucous street fight, participants throw powder and water at each other using the bright, exuberant colours to signify the start of spring, the power of love, and the generosity of humanity.

SOUNDS LIKE SOME SERIOUSLY MESSY FUN.

Just try to resist the truly jubilant spirit of the festival – everyone, and we mean everyone, comes together to play, laugh, forgive and give thanks. What's not to like?

31 AUGUST.

Las Bolas de Fuego, Nejapa, San Salvador, El Salvador

WE CAN'T HELP BUT NOTICE THAT TAKING PART IN THIS FESTIVAL LOOKS DECIDEDLY DANGEROUS.

There are some local festivities that we recommend you observe from a safe distance; if the balls of fire shooting back and forth, inches from participants' faces, hadn't already tipped you off, let us say – keep back, right back.

YOU DON'T HAVE TO TELL US TWICE.

What looks like an out-of-control street fight to the uninitiated is actually an established tradition for the people of Nejapa. In 1922 the town was threatened by the eruption of a nearby volcano, and as the volcano emitted flaming rocks, the townspeople interpreted it as their patron saint Jeronimo fighting the devil to save their homes. As a gesture of gratitude, the battle is now recreated in the streets each year with rival groups (usually exclusively young men) facing off and throwing fire at one another.

THAT'S CERTAINLY AN INTERESTING WAY TO SAY THANKS.

Despite the obvious health hazards there are surprisingly few injuries each year. That said, the sidelines are still the best place to be while the flames are going down.

WWW.ROCKETWAR.COM;
MARCH OR APRIL (EASTER).

Rouketopolemos (Rocket War), Vrontados, Chios, Greece

EASTER CELEBRATIONS IN GREECE CAN GET PRETTY LARGE, OR SO WE'VE HEARD.
It may well have been the Rocket War on the Greek Island of Chios that you've heard ringing in this important date on the Christian calendar.

ROCKET WAR DOESN'T SOUND LIKE YOUR TYPICAL EASTER CELEBRATION.
The story goes something along the lines of a traditional rivalry between two places of worship, and their respective congregations deciding to settle their differences by firing cannons at one another from opposing hilltops – all very Christian-spirited, right? Over the years it was sensibly decided that firing actual cannons was a tad too dangerous and the practice became what it is today. A massive display of large bottle rockets careening across the sky, the object of which is to hit the opposing church's belltower.

IT STILL SOUNDS LIKE CONTROLLED CHAOS.
Locals know that it's important to batten down the hatches and cover their houses and cars with a wire mesh cover before the battle begins. It's advisable for tourists to stay at a safe distance from the 'festivities', which is where the best views are anyway.

WWW.JNTO.GO.JP;
THIRD SATURDAY IN FEBRUARY.

Saidai-ji Eyo Hadaka Matsuri, Okayama, Japan

WE HAVEN'T SEEN ANYTHING QUITE LIKE THIS BEFORE.

It's fair to say that it's not every day you see close to 10,000 semi-naked Japanese men sprinting to a Shinto Temple to claim one of three small sticks believed to have sacred powers.

WE'RE SURE THERE'S A VERY GOOD REASON.

Well, there's a reason. According to legend, the ritual began hundreds of years ago when, as a way of expelling disease and misfortune from the land, the people believed getting a naked man to walk through an afflicted village would absorb the people's bad luck and evil. The unfortunate 'chosen one' or Shin-Otoko was then banished from society taking all the disease, bad luck, evil and misery with him. Over time the role of the Shin-Otoko has come to be seen as a fortunate one.

HOW DO THEY FIGURE THAT?

Who knows, but the festival now draws huge crowds of loin-clothed men vying for the title of 'lucky man'. To win the crown, a competitor must run through a pool of freezing water before frantically jostling to retrieve the *shingi* (sacred stick) after it has been tossed from the platform of a temple. We recommend standing to the side to see it all go down.

WWW.SONGKRAN2014.COM;

13–15 APRIL.

Songkran Water Festival, Bangkok, Thailand

WATER FIGHT! LIKE YOU'VE NEVER SEEN BEFORE.

The Songkran Festival, which sees in the new year in Thailand, is celebrated all over the country, but the most crowd-soaking fun and fervour takes place in the nation's capital.

WE'RE NOT MAKING THE CONNECTION BETWEEN NEW YEAR'S DAY AND WATER FIGHTING.

Oh come on – the connection is fun, pure and simple! For three days in April (the hottest month in Thailand) Thais line the streets and throw bowls of cooling water or fire super-soakers at anything that moves. Some believe that the water washes away bad luck so that good luck can usher in the new year. We advise you to get into the spirit because there is no possible way of escaping getting totally saturated.

WHERE'S THE BEST PART OF THE CITY TO GET IN ON THE ACTION?

Try Silom, where a whole 5km section of road is sectioned off by fire trucks at either end so revellers don't have to negotiate traffic. Be warned, the fire trucks are armed with fully loaded hoses and they're not afraid to use them.

Art and culture

WWW.AGITAGUEDA.COM;
JULY (EXACT DATES VARY).

AgitAgueda Art Festival, Agueda, Portugal

WOW, THE UMBRELLAS IN THE SKY.
One of the most recognisable symbols of this vibrant Portuguese festival is the installation of hundreds of colourful umbrellas suspended above one of the city's streets. Other parts of the urban landscape, like park benches, stairs, and power poles, are also painted in colourful examples of street art, creating an enchanted atmosphere.

WHAT'S IT ALL IN AID OF?
The festival aims to promote new musical and artistic projects with the 'Talentos AgitAgueda', a competition for emerging artists. As well as new hopefuls there are many established national and international acts that grace the stage.

DO WE HAVE TIME TO CHECK IT ALL OUT?
The festivities extend over three weeks so there's plenty of time to pack it all in. Many of the musical acts perform in the main tent, which is free. And there's nothing stopping you from walking around the streets to see all the amazing outdoor installations, murals and sculptures.

WWW.EDFRINGE.COM;

AUGUST.

Edinburgh Fringe Festival, Scotland, UK

THIS IS ALL WEIRD PERFORMANCE ART, ISN'T IT?

This is the granddaddy of performance art festivals and you can bet on seeing some weird and wonderful acts over the month it's held. But it's not all Shakespearean plays performed by dangerously drunk actors, and grim, ironic, post-modern, pre-future fairytales. The entertainment on offer is unbelievably diverse: musicals, kids' shows, dance, circus, cabaret...

... I THINK I REALLY JUST WANT A LAUGH.

... and comedy. The Fringe has a strong humour focus; you'll find a laugh or two for sure. Rowan Atkinson, Eddie Izzard and Billy Connolly made names for themselves here.

THAT DOESN'T SOUND FRINGEY AT ALL!

Maybe not at their current levels of fame. But here there's some genuinely ground-breaking stuff going on. You're likely to experience acts that might not make it into more mainstream arts festivals – at least, not until Fringe-found fame opens those kinds of doors.

WWW.ICEFESTIVALHARBIN.COM;
5 JANUARY FOR ONE MONTH.

Ice and Snow Sculpture Festival, Harbin, China

THERE ARE A FEW OF THESE ICE FESTIVALS AROUND THE WORLD.
As with many things in China, this one is supersized, and while big isn't always better, it's hard to argue with the sight of the almighty sculptures on display.

WHAT SORT OF SNOW AND ICE CREATIONS ARE WE LIKELY TO SEE?
What aren't you going to see? The Harbin festival has four different display parks all packed with larger-than-life sculptural wonders carved from ice and colourfully lit up like winter fairgrounds. There are cartoon-like characters, animals, mythical creatures and architectural marvels, like a replica of the Great Wall of China and a soaring edifice standing 46 metres in height, to mention just a few.

THE FESTIVAL LASTS A WHOLE MONTH! WON'T WE TIRE OF WALKING AROUND LOOKING AT ICE MONUMENTS?
Try getting in on some ice action by having a go on the ice slides or riding a sled around some of the monuments. Or, if you're really brave, put your name forward to compete in the annual ice swim. Yes, it is exactly as it sounds.

South by Southwest, Austin, Texas, USA

WHAT'S GOING ON HERE – IS IT A MUSIC FESTIVAL? A FILM FESTIVAL? A COMEDY FESTIVAL?

All of the above and more. SXSW runs for nine days in March and totally overruns the Austin city streets with new music, art, comedy and movies, along with speaking panels packed with a who's who of pop culture, new media and the arts.

SOUNDS LIKE WE'RE GOING TO HAVE A FULL DANCE CARD.

There are more than 2000 different acts from all over the world so you might want to think about some pre-planning. Either that or you could stumble around town and see what kind of Next Big Thing you can bump into. SXSW is famous for showcasing up-and-coming talent so be prepared to add bragging rights to your Twitter feed.

AND THE SPEAKING PANEL PART – WHAT'S THAT ABOUT?

There are all kinds of interactive panels on issues as diverse as design, technology, urban strategy, fashion, broadcasting, travel, and gaming; each panel is packed with carefully recruited expert keynote speakers all with reputations for being game-changers and visionaries. Expect wall-to-wall digital hipsters.

WWW.SUNDANCE.ORG;
JANUARY.

Sundance Film Festival, Utah, USA

AH, WE HAVE TO LINE UP WITH THE CELEBRITIES IN THEIR SKI GEAR FOR THIS ONE.

Despite being a showcase for up-and-coming films, this festival has always had Hollywood's attention – its founder and patron, Robert Redford, being one of LA's old-school stars.

WE'RE NOT REALLY INTO THE HOLLYWOOD BLOCKBUSTERS.

Don't worry, despite the tinsel-town connections, and its reputation as one of the biggest film festivals in the United States, there is a firm commitment to independent and up-and-coming film-makers.

THE NEXT BIG THINGS?

The festival has given a start to some of the world's most highly respected film-makers, like Quentin Tarantino, Steven Soderbergh, Darren Aronofsky, Jim Jarmusch and Robert Rodriguez, and has launched films like *The Blair Witch Project*, *Donnie Darko*, *Napoleon Dynamite* and *Saw* onto the international stage.

HOW DO THEY KEEP IT REAL?

Anyone can enter their film in one of the many categories available. There's a staggeringly popular documentary category, narrative feature films, short films and even virtual reality projects. You're guaranteed to see something unique.

WWW.WNFESTIVAL.COM;
MAY TO JULY.

White Nights Festival, St Petersburg, Russia

THE SUMMER MAY BE SHORT IN RUSSIA BUT THEY KNOW HOW TO MAKE THE MOST OF IT IN ST PETERSBURG.

Do they! In what should be described as a series of many major artistic events and not just one festival, White Nights runs over the longest days of the year and features a staggeringly varied array of performances and exhibitions.

WHAT SORT OF THINGS CAN WE EXPECT?

There is classical music, opera, dance, film, circus acts, comedy, theatre, sculpture, jazz concerts and myriad other performing arts pieces on show. Many performances are outdoors, so strolling around the city centre or along the banks of the River Neva you're likely to catch a free show.

GIVE US A COUPLE OF MUST-SEES.

One of the most justifiably popular events is the Scarlet Sails – the recreation of a child's storybook. A giant crimson-tailed longship is sailed up the River Neva towards the Tsar's palace, with accompanying fireworks and lightshows. This spectacle draws crowds in their millions. Also, make sure to be at the opening of the drawbridge at least once – a street party erupts at 2am each night the drawbridge is retracted.

WWW.BODYPAINTING-FESTIVAL.COM;

JULY.

World Body Painting Festival, Pörtschach, Austria

A STEP ABOVE THE FACE-PAINTING STALL AT OUR LOCAL FETE.

This is a go-to destination for anyone who has ever been interested in body art. There is awe-inspiring body painting on show as well as airbrush and special effects artists working their magic. In some cases, it's hard to even believe that there's a human being underneath that paintwork.

THERE'S QUITE A BUZZ GOING ON – IS THAT A DJ ON STAGE?

Over the years, the body painting festival has broadened its horizons to become a self-proclaimed 'multicultural, multimedia open air space' and that's why you can experience five different zones with a host of DJs playing anything from reggae to electronica, to dancehall to hip hop. There's even a stretch of beach dedicated to activities for the kids and a whole market zone with fashion, craft and jewellery.

WHERE CAN WE SEE THE BEST OF THE BODY PAINTING?

The best body artists from over 50 countries around the world are on show, so everywhere you look there are stunning pieces of art. However, for something a bit different, stick around until the evening show of the best UV body paint, spectacularly lit up under lights.

Calm and tranquil

WWW.LANTERNFLOATINGHAWAII.COM;
MEMORIAL DAY IN THE USA (LATE MAY).

Floating Lantern Festival, Ala Moana Beach, Hawaii

NOW THIS IS A PRETTY SETTING FOR A FESTIVAL. WHAT'S GOING ON?

Part memorial day, part celebration of cultural harmony, this serene lantern festival starts with a sounding of the *pu*, a Hawaiian conch shell. The call of the *pu* sanctifies the beach for the beginning of the festival.

AND ONCE THIS BEAUTIFUL BEACH HAS BEEN BLESSED, WHAT HAPPENS THEN?

A series of local customs and rituals designed to call people together in peace and harmony. There's a performance of the hula and an *Oli* chant.

AND THE LANTERN PART?

There are six main lanterns which carry the prayers offered for victims of war (that's the memorial bit). Then there are prayers for those who have died as a result of natural and man-made disasters, famine, disease, and water-related accidents. We're not entirely sure why prayers are said for these victims exclusively, but we're pretty sure you could get away with floating your own lantern for whoever you want. In the end, it's the sight of hundreds of candlelit lanterns floating over the water under the setting sun that brings beauty and peace all around.

The International Highline Meeting Festival, Monte Piana, Italy

IT DOESN'T LOOK LIKE THERE ARE MANY PEOPLE HERE...

Look up.

WHOAH, THAT'S A NEW ONE.

The festival goers that are suspended hundreds of feet above the ground in those colourful hammocks are called slackers, and they're not your usual festival slackers; these guys earned their name from the slack wire helping to prevent them plunging to their deaths. The fiesta is a chance for lovers of the sport to meet up in a totally non-competitive environment.

WHAT IF WE PREFER THE VIEW OF THE DOLOMITES FROM SOLID GROUND?

Completely understandable; the aim of the get-together is to not only give enthusiasts a chance to hang out (boom boom) but to gently introduce newbies to the sport. Don't feel pressured to get high (bam) – the festival organisers put on musical entertainment, an outdoor cinema, food stalls and yoga lessons for those not into the high life. At night there's a dance party that even the slackers get in on.

FEBRUARY OR MARCH.

Pingxi Lantern Festival, Pingxi, Taiwan

THIS LOOKS PRETTY.
It's a stunningly luminous sight. Close to 200,000 lanterns are released into the night sky at the start of the new Lunar Year.

BEAUTIFUL, BUT WHY? AND WHY HERE?
According to ancient legend, the lanterns were originally lit to let Pingxi villagers, who had fled their homes under the threat of outlaw raids, know that it was safe to return. Over the hundreds and hundreds of years, the lanterns have come to represent a release of bad habits and an aspiration to achieve positive ideals.

SO WE ALL TREK AN HOUR OUT OF TAIPEI TO GET INVOLVED?
Just you and 80,000 of your closest friends. It's an extremely popular way to see out the old Chinese year, so expect to jostle for space to release your good luck lantern.

IS IT WORTH BRAVING THE CROWDS?
The radiant light of the lanterns against the dark night is a spectacle not to be understated. Add to this beautiful sight the goodwill and optimistic vibe of the participants, and you have a night you'll never forget.

Foodie

Bordeaux Fête le Vin, Bordeaux, France

WE SENSE A WINNING COMBINATION OF LOCATION AND THEME HERE.

The viticulture gods do shine down on this UNESCO World Heritage site at the end of June each year. With an architecturally stunning setting and world-famous vineyards surrounding the town, this fabulous festival draws in wine aficionados from all corners of the globe.

WINE TASTING IN BORDEAUX? WELL, WE GUESS SOMEONE HAS TO DO IT.

You will most certainly not be alone; this shindig is known as one of the biggest wine festivals in the world and while the wine is first and foremost, the four-day fiesta includes barrel-rolling competitions, live music, fireworks displays and sound and light shows each night. That is, of course, if you get tired of all the tippling.

LET'S GET STARTED THEN.

The festival sets up on a two kilometre stretch of road between the historical old town and the river, with a string of tasting pavilions featuring more than 80 appellations from Bordeaux and the Aquitaine region. Make your way to the water.

WWW.MADFEED.CO;

LATE AUGUST.

MAD Symposium, Copenhagen, Denmark

A SYMPOSIUM? SOUNDS SERIOUS.

When famed Danish chef, Rene Redzepi (of Noma note), pulled the symposium together for the first time in 2011, we imagine he was hoping that everyone would take his efforts seriously. And they did: in the short time that the symposium has been running it has garnered a reputation as 'the Food World's G-20'.

A CHEF MASH UP?

The philosophy behind MAD is 'to expand knowledge of food to make every meal a better meal... Good cooking and a healthy environment can and should go hand-in-hand'.

So yes, there's a healthy contingent of eager chefs, but the symposium draws in many others from the food industry, including farmers, food journalists, suppliers and food-service professionals.

DELICIOUS INSPIRATION.

The cast of guest speakers reads like a who's who of the international restaurant world. Think David Chang, Albert Adria, Alain Ducasse, to name just a few – so you would be hard-pressed to come away from the festival without a mind packed with new culinary ideas.

WWW.MAINELOBSTERFESTIVAL.COM;

EARLY AUGUST.

Maine Lobster Festival, Rockland, New England, USA

THIS LOOKS LIKE A TASTY WAY TO SPEND A DAY.

What started as a community initiative to boost interest in local seafood has become a world-regarded festival celebrating the superior quality of the region's marine produce. Tasty indeed.

DO WE ALL SIT AROUND GORGING OURSELVES ON LOBSTER?

And butter – don't forget the butter. Each year, close to 10,000 kilos of these delicious crustaceans are cooked up with over 750 kilos of melted butter. We are not even kidding. Luckily, if you feel the need to burn off some of this extravagant eating, the festival organisers have cooked up some seafood-themed activities so you can justify round two.

NOT JUST EATING COMPETITIONS?

Break up the gorging by joining the joggers in the 10km road race; or have a go at the Lobster Crate Race, where competitors hop from crate to crate across the open water; or just cheer on the festival's reigning Sea Goddess at the Maine Street Parade. There are also cooking demonstrations and competitions, so you can take a little lobster inspiration from the locals back home with you.

WWW.OKTOBERFEST.DE;
MID TO LATE SEPTEMBER.

Oktoberfest, Munich, Germany

AH BEER, GLORIOUS BEER.
If you happen to be partial to the amber ale, as millions of us are, then Oktoberfest is known to you. If you go to join the fun, you'll discover it's the beating heart of the beer-swilling world.

TELL US IT'S NOT ALL BOOZY LADS STUMBLING AROUND IN LEDERHOSEN.
Over six million visitors turn up to be a part of the festivities so chances are you'll run into a few boozy lads but they won't dominate the fun.

WE IMAGINE THAT WE MIGHT BE NURSING A HANGOVER AT SOME STAGE.
In that case, eat yourself out of a hole with traditional treats like *hendl* (roast chicken), *schweinebraten* (roast pork), or *schweinshaxe* (grilled ham hock).

ALRIGHT, WE'RE BACK ON THE HORSE.
Before you get into doing your bit with the nearly eight million litres of beer that is drunk here each year, have a go on the amusement rides and sideshow games. Your eye might be slightly out later.

WWW.CORPORATE.SOBEFEST.COM;
FEBRUARY OR MARCH.

South Beach Food and Wine Festival, Miami Beach, Florida, USA

FOOD, WINE, THE BEACH – THESE ARE SOME WINNING INGREDIENTS ALREADY.
This food and wine extravaganza has been running for 15 years and attracts foodie superstars from not only the United States but all over the world. This kind of culinary clout draws in more than 65,000 guests who partake in over 80 different events over five, flavour-packed days.

THE REAL QUESTION HERE IS, 'DO WE GET TO TASTE?'
Absolutely. Outside of cooking demonstrations by celebrity chefs such as the likes of Bobby Flay and Martha Stewart, there are tasting events like the luxurious Oyster Bash, top notch fruits of the sea with matched wines, or the best burger competition – where the crowd gets a say in who gets crowned best burger chef for the festival.

I CAN'T DECIDE WHAT TO EAT.
If the veritable smorgasbord of events is too much to take in, then get into the Grand Tasting Village on the last day. There's a little bit of everything on offer so you can stroll and sample at your own pace.

WWW.SPIRITOFSPEYSIDE.COM;
APRIL OR MAY.

Spirit of Speyside Whisky Festival, Speyside, Scotland, UK

THIS MUST BE PARADISE.

If your idea of paradise involves more whisky than you could poke a caber at, then yes, this is paradise.

A CABER? WHAT?

You know, the caber toss? Never mind. The point is that you're in Scotland, and is there anything more Scottish than whisky? And this is where the spirit comes to life, a five-day celebration of the art, craft and business of making and drinking the water of life.

I'VE ALREADY BOOKED A TICKET.

You won't be disappointed. The festival takes place in the towns, villages and 50 distilleries of Speyside, with some 400 events over its five days. There are distillery tours and tastings, talks, whisky fairs, fine dining dinners, live music...

MY MOUTH IS WATERING.

It's a truly satisfying festival, blending single malt with the singular beauty of rural Scotland and its convivial hospitality. You'll go for the whisky but stay for Speyside itself. Ok, and the whisky. But you'll stay, that much is certain.

Just one big party

WWW.AMSTERDAMGAYPRIDE.NL;
LATE AUGUST TO EARLY, JULY.

Amsterdam Gay Pride/Europride, Amsterdam, The Netherlands

THERE ARE GAY PRIDE PARADES ALL OVER THE WORLD - WHY AMSTERDAM?

Trying to choose the best gay pride party in the world is kind of like choosing a favourite child. There are so many cities that turn on a tremendous event – Sydney, San Francisco, London, New York, the list goes on. However, Amsterdam gets the vote having rolled the event into the supersized 'Europride', a three-week long LGBT celebratory extravaganza.

THREE WEEKS! THAT'S A HELL OF A PRIDE.

If three weeks off work is too much to ask, make sure you're there for the last weekend (early August) – that's when most of the major events take place.

WHAT'S IN STORE FOR US AS PART OF THESE FINAL FESTIVITIES?

Street parties, the Drag Queen Olympics, the Canal Parade, the Funhouse dance party, and the enormous Pride Closing Party. Some events are divided into either gay or lesbian, and some are themed, like the Bear Necessities, but the vibe is generally inclusive and fun for all.

WWW.BURNINGMAN.ORG;

LAST MONDAY OF AUGUST TO FIRST MONDAY IN SEPTEMBER.

Burning Man, Black Rock Desert, Nevada, USA

ISN'T THIS A BUNCH OF HIPPIES DANCING AROUND IN THE DESERT?

We prefer to think of it as 70,000 free-spirits bringing their creative energy together to enjoy one of the world's biggest arts and culture festivals.

RIGHT ON.

No kidding. Since its organic inception in 1986, when founder Larry Harvey and friends spontaneously burnt an effigy of a man on a San Francisco beach, the festival has grown into a mind-boggling plethora of artistic expression, from supersized sculptures to interactive performances. Each night is a flaming, kaleidoscopic circus of light, sound, music and dancing.

IT MIGHT BE TIME TO LET GO OF ALL OUR TRADITIONAL, MATERIALISTIC HANG-UPS AND JOIN THE FUN.

That's the spirit. The festival is not a spectator experience: be prepared to dive headlong into costumes and connections. Most attendees join a themed camp and help out by constructing the realisation of the camp's ethos. Past camps have included concepts like Playasos, a light-hearted community of people who love spontaneous play and exploration; or '...and then there's only LOVE', for the 'romantics' who look forward to meeting up in the Orgy Dome. For real.

WWW.CARNEVALE.VENEZIA.IT;
LATE JANUARY TO EARLY FEBRUARY.

Carnevale, Venice, Italy

OLD-WORLD, MASKED ELEGANCE.
Aside from dapper gondoliers cruising the city's canals, there are few images as iconic to Italy's water-circled city as the masked partygoers at the world-famous Venice Carnevale. Officially recognised as a festival from the Renaissance period, Carnevale was a licence to indulge in heedless pleasure, with masks to protect participant's identities. However, when all this licentiousness became too much, the King of Austria outlawed the festival and it was only in the 20th century that Venetians brought the party back..

SO DECADENCE IS BACK ON THE TABLE?
With bells on. More than three million visitors crowd Venice's cobbled streets during Carnevale for the chance to be a part of the festivities.

MUST WE COME MASKED?
Not all participants are masked, but donning a disguise certainly amps up the fun. If you're stuck for inspiration, check out the costume parade on stage in St Mark's Square – the winners each day go head to head for the title of festival finest on the last day of celebrations.

WWW.RIO-CARNIVAL.NET;

LATE FEBRUARY.

Carnival, Rio de Janeiro, Brazil

JUST WAIT WHILE WE GRAB OUR BEDAZZLED FEATHER HEADDRESS.

That's the spirit. There's nothing for it but to throw yourself wholeheartedly into the hedonism that is the world's biggest, brightest, loudest carnival street party.

THESE BRAZILIANS CERTAINLY KNOW HOW TO PARTY.

So much so that the prospect of 40 days of good behaviour over Lent sends locals into a last-ditch party planning frenzy. Before everyone is expected to better themselves, they let it all hang out with music, massive parades, lots of drinking and non-stop dancing.

CAN WE GET INVOLVED EVEN IF WE CAN'T CARRY OFF THE WHOLE FEATHERED-BIKINI LOOK?

So long as you're prepared to move to a samba beat, no one is going to stop you. Most visitors join in on a *bloco* (street party) where a band of drummers leads people through the streets in a non-stop dance off. You may be asked to colour-coordinate your t-shirt but won't be required to strip down to next to nothing. Be warned, however: the music may make you do things you never dreamed of. Anything goes.

WWW.CHINATOWNFESTIVALS.SG;

EARLY FEBRUARY.

Chinese New Year, Singapore

IF IT'S CHINESE NEW YEAR WE'RE CELEBRATING WHY AREN'T WE CELEBRATING IT IN CHINA?

It's true that some of the biggest, loudest and longest Chinese New Year celebrations happen in China, but with these come the crowds. The family focus on Chinese New Year in China sees the world's largest human migration surging towards Beijing, creating deadlocked human traffic jams, which kind of take the fun out of the festival.

SO SINGAPORE WILL GIVE US THE SPACE TO ENJOY OURSELVES?

Don't expect empty streets – partygoers pile into Singapore to join in the extraordinary mix of old and new traditional celebrations. The Chingay Parade is the largest street and float parade in all of Asia, with dancing dragons, stilt walkers, acrobats and lion walkers. At the River Hongbao you'll see traditional song and dance performances and a release of giant lanterns.

TELL US THERE ARE FIREWORKS? THERE'S GOT TO BE FIREWORKS.

No Chinese New Year celebration is complete without a totally over-the-top fireworks display and Singapore certainly turns on the pyrotechnics. Expect a blinding display that turns night into a colourful day.

**BEGINS 30 SEPTEMBER AND RUNS EACH WEEKEND
THROUGH TO EARLY DECEMBER.**

Feast of San Jeronimo, Masaya, Nicaragua

THIS IS LIKE A NEVER-ENDING STREET PARTY.

This party has the honour of calling itself the longest festival in Nicaragua. The celebrations kick off when townspeople carry an enormously heavy effigy of Saint Jerome from the church through the streets of the village.

NOT TO BE A DOWNER BUT, IS THAT IT?

It wouldn't really be much of a party if that was the end of things. Following the street parade for Saint Jerome, the people of Masaya recreate the Torovenado parade that honours the Nicaraguan Saint Silvester – this other-worldly street march has participants dressed in all manner of weird and wonderful costumes – from unusual animals and folkloric demons to caricatures of famous Nicaraguans. There is music, dancing and food, and at night the whole thing turns into one huge party.

WHY DOES THIS HAPPEN IN MASAYA?

This village is known as the folklore capital of Nicaragua, which is why the party goes on and on for weeks and weeks after the initial parade. In fact, there's a party every weekend for three months following the last day in September.

WWW.MARDIGRASNEWORLEANS.COM;

LATE FEBRUARY.

Mardi Gras, New Orleans, Louisiana, USA

SOME TOWNS JUST KNOW HOW TO THROW A GOOD PARTY.

The city of New Orleans just can't help itself, and during the annual Mardi Gras it's a no holds barred, free-for-all, fun time. The motto of the festival is 'les bons temp rouler' which translates to 'let the good times roll'.

WHY MARDI GRAS AND WHY HERE?

Mardi Gras is French for 'fat Tuesday', which, for those who observe the Christian calendar, is a sign it's time to go all out before Lent begins, when it's expected you'll reign it in and

behave yourself. The French are credited with bringing Mardi Gras to New Orleans, but it's the mix with the mystic and pagan 'krewes' that gives Mardi Gras in New Orleans its edge.

CAN WE JOIN A KREWE?

The krewes are exemplified by different parades which actually represent different neighbourhoods or local communities. They're themed and highly decorated with epic floats and awesome costumes. If you're a visitor and not part of a krewe, you'll have to settle for epic and awesome dancing, drinking, music and mounds of the famous colourful beads.

WWW.STPATRICKSFESTIVAL.IE;

17 MARCH.

St Patrick's Day, Dublin, Ireland

LIKE THE IRISH NEED AN EXCUSE FOR A GUINNESS AND A GOOD TIME.

Friday is a good excuse for a Guinness. St Patrick's Day is the best excuse for Ireland's biggest knees-up of the year.

THROUGH A BOOZY HAZE WE CAN ALMOST MAKE OUT THE HISTORICAL SIGNIFICANCE.

The Feast of Saint Patrick, Ireland's foremost patron saint, is held every year on the anniversary of his death, to commemorate his influence and the arrival of Christianity in Ireland. Traditional Lenten restrictions on eating and drinking are relaxed for the day – hence the rush to the bar.

ASIDE FROM THE DRINKING, WHAT DOES OUR ST PATRICK'S DAY HAVE IN STORE?

Expect to see lively street parades with marching bands, the military, fire brigades, cultural organisations and others, often swathed in green. There are well-attended church services and day-long festivities with traditional Irish music and dancing sessions. It is customary to end the day by putting a shamrock in the bottom of your glass of beer or whiskey and toasting to the Saint, Ireland and those around you. Swallow the shamrock or toss it over your shoulder for good luck.

WWW.UPHELLYAA.ORG;

LAST TUESDAY IN JANUARY.

Up Helly Aa Fire Festival, Lerwick, Scotland

IT'S WILD AND WOOLLY UP HERE ON THE SHETLAND ISLES.
Which might explain this festival's obsession with fire. Sitting at the same latitude as the bottom half of Greenland, the locals know all about the cold, so don't expect any sympathy if you're a sensitive mainlander.

OK, WE WON'T LET THE WEATHER GET THE BETTER OF US. BUT WE STILL DON'T UNDERSTAND WHAT'S GOING ON.
It's easy to see why the whole thing comes across as just a wee bit crazy – rowdy local men dressed as Vikings, tramping shoulder-to-shoulder through the centre of Lerwick carrying flaming torches. It's a fiery, boozy, boisterous celebration of the island's Viking heritage and cultural ancestry, which culminates in the burning of a life-sized replica of a longship.

FORGET THE FIRE, IT ALL SOUNDS LIKE IT'S TESTOSTERONE-FUELLED TO US.
The parade is men-only (must be a Viking thing) but don't think that women won't get in on the partying that happens after the bonfire. The whole thing only lasts 24 hours, but it's non-stop from start to finish.

Music

WWW.SPLASH.COACHELLA.COM;
TWO WEEKENDS IN APRIL.

Coachella, California, USA

FINALLY, A FESTIVAL FOR ALL THE FORGOTTEN RICH AND FAMOUS KIDS OF CALIFORNIA.

I know, right! Poor dears. Anyone who isn't a supermodel or international 'it' girl might feel like they've stumbled onto the set of an advertisement for Coca Cola. Don't worry, though. The extras get to have just as much fun without the paparazzi tailing their every move.

SO THE CROWD IS YOUNG AND PAINFULLY COOL – WHAT ABOUT THE MUSIC?

If you're over 40, you'll struggle to recognise a majority of the names, unless of course you're one of those middle-aged hipsters; then you'll recognise names like Beachhouse, Flume, Gary Clarke Jnr, and Purity Ring. There are hundreds of established and up-and-coming acts that perform in a wonderfully eclectic variety of genres. Think hip-hop, rock, indie and electronic dance.

WE MIGHT BE TOO OLD FOR THIS.

Oh get out! In 2016, the organisers rolled out Guns N' Roses as a headline act. Rock on, oldies!

Glastonbury Festival, Somerset, UK

BETTER PACK OUR OBLIGATORY GUMBOOTS.
Each year, Glastonbury makes the headlines with images of British celebrities trudging through the mud in gumboots and hot pants. However, despite the cheap tabloid shots, this long-running festival maintains a focus on social activism and environmental issues, as well as a serious emphasis on music and the performing arts.

WE'VE HEARD THE HEADLINE ACTS DRAW A BIG CROWD.
It has a reputation as the biggest greenfield festival in the world – since the inaugural get-together in 1970, it now runs over five days and attracts more than 175,000 attendees.

THESE MUST BE SOME SERIOUSLY POPULAR POP STARS.
Glastonbury brings out the big guns – headline artists over the years have included such rock and pop behemoths as David Bowie, Van Morrison, The Smiths, Radiohead, The White Stripes, Neil Young and U2. In more recent years, the festival has widened its musical appreciation to include rap and R&B artists like Jay Z and Dizzie Rascal, and on some of the smaller stages you'll be treated to up-and-coming acts before they hit the big time.

WWW.MONTREALJAZZFEST.COM;
LATE JUNE TO EARLY JULY.

Montreal International Jazz Festival, Montreal, Quebec, Canada

SO THIS IS WHERE WE GO IF WE WANT SOME SMOOTH JAZZ?

That's right. Each year, Montreal sees the largest collection of cool cats in the world. And if you don't believe us, take the Guinness Book of World Records' word for it – they list the festival as the world's biggest jazz fest; with around 3000 artists from more than 30 countries performing more than 650 concerts to over 2.5 million visitors. Now those are some seriously cool stats.

HOW WILL WE FIT IT ALL IN?

There are shows in big concert halls and popular clubs, but many of the performances are free and outdoors. Part of the city's downtown district is closed to traffic for 10 days so that shows can be staged in the streets and city parks, so no one misses out.

WHO CAN WE HOPE TO SEE?

If past line-ups are anything to go by you'll get a who's who of who's hot. The festival has featured legends like Leonard Cohen, Ella Fitzgerald, Paco de Lucia, John McLaughlin and Keith Jarrett in the past, and recent headliners have included k.d. lang, Diana Ross, Chick Corea and Joey Alexander.

WWW.RHYTHMANDVINES.CO.NZ;

29 DECEMBER – 1 JANUARY.

Rhythm and Vines, Gisbourne, New Zealand

THERE'S A LOT OF COMPETITION FOR NEW YEAR'S EVE FESTIVITIES – WHY HERE?

If you want bragging rights over your buddies in the slower upper reaches of the globe, then feel free to boast about being way ahead of them in seeing the first the sunrise of the New Year.

AND WHAT'S GOING TO KEEP US AWAKE TILL THE GLORIOUS MORNING?

When Rhythm and Vines first kicked off in 2003, it had one stage and 1800 guests. These days, over 25,000 festival goers flood in to Gisbourne to check out the many musical stages hosting big-name international acts like NERD, Tinie Tempah, Tame Impala, Mark Ronson, as well as home-grown legends like Shihad and The Naked and Famous. In 2014, R&V introduced the Arcadia Spectacular, a fiery performance space based on Glastonbury's famous fire-breathing stage. There's also a stand-up comic stage for a little light relief.

THIS CAN'T BE JUST A ONE-NIGHT-STAND!

The festival is a three-day camping extravaganza with a range of different site options available. Our pick: the two-person eco tent provided by the organisers which looks a bit like a cardboard cubby box. Just bring your sleeping bags and plonk your recyclable fort in amongst the vines.

WWW.ROSKILDE-FESTIVAL.DK;
LATE JUNE TO EARLY JULY.

Roskilde Music Festival, Roskilde, Denmark

WHAT MAKES A MUSIC FESTIVAL IN A SMALL TOWN IN DENMARK SO SPECIAL?

Who knows exactly why Roskilde became the biggest North European culture and music festival. We do know that being a completely not-for-profit event certainly helps. All the proceeds of the festival go towards charitable initiatives in support of children and young people. The initiatives are entirely independent and are not limited to Europe. This said, though, it has something to do with rock and roll.

AH YES, ROCK AND ROLL. GETS US EVERY TIME.

Since 1971 in this case. From the early days of live bands on one stage, the festival has evolved to include different arts and culture-themed camps, like the Street Camp which features some of the world's best skaters and games of street soccer and volleyball; the Rising City, which showcases up-and-coming artistic and musical talent; and the Graffiti Zone, a huge area filled with graffiti, murals, and other art installations.

YOU HAD BETTER GET AROUND TO TELLING US ABOUT THE MUSIC.

Nine stages with over 180 international and local acts. It's a star-studded line-up that includes artists of the moment like Tame Impala and Wiz Khalifa, and musical legends like Neil Young and the Red Hot Chili Peppers.

HTTPS://SONAR.ES;
JUNE.

Sonar, Barcelona, Spain

THE DOOF DOOF COMES TO TOWN.
Don't come expecting your run-of-the-mill dance club acts: Sonar brings you back to the future of electronic music. The performances are a mash-up of everything that is hot in the sound scene. You can expect to see some familiar names showcasing new adventures and some artists who are so fresh they haven't yet been defined.

OK, LET'S DO SOME TIME TRAVEL – TAKE US TO THE FUTURE OF SOUND.
Sonar doesn't just stick to the standard 'artist on stage in front of audience' formula. The festival mixes it up with interesting exhibition and installation spaces in which to showcase electronic and advanced music sounds. Take for example the L'Auditori, a venue which is traditionally used for orchestras but which substitutes strings for sub-woofers when Sonar is in town.

GIVE US A HINT AT THE KIND OF HEROES AND PIONEERS WE CAN EXPECT TO SEE.
The festival-kick started in 1994 but it wasn't till 1997 that it really started to attract some big electronic dance music artists. The line-up from that year lists the crème de la crème of EDM with names like Daft Punk, Kraftwerk, Kruder & Dorfmeister, Deep Dish, Herbert, Death in Vegas, and Coldcut. In 2016 the acts included Santigold, Underground Resistence, Richie Hawtin and James Rhodes.

WWW.SPLENDOURINTHEGRASS.COM;

JULY.

Splendour in the Grass, Byron Bay, Australia

I DON'T WANT TO GO ALL LITERARY ON YOU, BUT THAT'S A POEM NOT A FESTIVAL.

Nice one, nerd. But yes, this winter music festival has Wordsworth to thank for its name. Make no mistake though; the genuine splendour of this festival is all about top international and local acts making their way to the spectacularly beautiful, far north New South Wales coast.

I WAS THINKING IT WAS A HIPPY GET-TOGETHER.

Byron Bay has a long history of celebrating the alternative lifestyle, so you may well be exposed to a number of free-spirited forms of fun. And a good helping of vegetarian food to boot. But the music spans both mainstream and alternative rock/pop – the kind of headlines you expect to see at the world's top music festivals.

HANG ON... FAR NORTH NSW? THAT SOUNDS... ISOLATED.

It's not an urban festival, no doubt. But factor in the pristine natural environment, awesome beaches and a line-up that has seen artists like Coldplay, Kanye West and The Strokes make the trek, you'd be crazy to not have this gig on your music festival bucket list.

WWW.WOMADELAIDE.COM.AU;

MARCH.

WOMADelaide, Adelaide, South Australia, Australia

UM, ADELAIDE – NOT YOUR TYPICAL AUSSIE TOURIST DRAWCARD.

The state capital of South Australia doesn't often hit world headlines, but with this perennially popular world-music festival it steals the show.

WHAT'S WOMADELAIDE ALL ABOUT?

If you can beat it, strum it, blow it, shake it, dance to it, sing with it, then you might find it here. This is a festival that showcases a staggeringly broad variety of music from all over the world. Over the course of its four days, festival-goers get treated to such a diverse selection of musical styles they'll feel like they've been on an international tour of tunes.

LIKE WHAT?

Here's a sample of the eclectic acts that have previously been on show: Nusrat Fateh Ali Khan, Peter Gabriel, Gil Scott Heron, Fat Freddy's Drop, Miriam Makeba, and the Master Drummers of Burundi. There's dance, rock, pop, jazz, folk, country, classical and genres that you've never even heard of before. The whole melange of musical tastes combines to create a warm and inclusive vibe of festival revellers who are open-minded and ready for the next big world-music thing.

Off the wall

WWW.AIRGUITARWORLDCHAMPIONSHIPS.COM;
LATE AUGUST.

Air Guitar World Championships, Oulu, Finland

IS THIS JUST GOING TO BE LIKE EVERY STUDENT HOUSE-SHARE ON A SATURDAY NIGHT?

You can expect a superior standard to your mate Dave's beer-fuelled rendition of 'Back in Black'. The competitors who make it to this, the holy grail of air guitar competitions, take their craft very seriously.

HOW SERIOUSLY?

If you're in any doubt as to the earnestness of the ideals of the competition, then have a read of the organisers' ideology. These peaceful rockers believe that if everyone in the world played air guitar, wars would end, climate change would stop and all bad things would disappear. Now that's got to be worth a riff, right?

HOW DO WE GET IN ON THE FUN?

Choose your song, practise like crazy, then send in a one-minute edited clip of your best effort. Or work your way through your national ranks. Be sure to play with technical accuracy and unbridled passion. Remember that your instrument must be invisible, although it can be either electric or acoustic in make (believe), and you are not allowed any air roadies or air back-up bands – that would, of course, be a totally unfair advantage.

WWW.MUDFESTIVAL.OR.KR;

MID TO LATE JULY.

Boryeong Mud Festival, Boryeong, South Korea

TIME TO GET DOWN AND DIRTY?

You got that right. Many Koreans believe that the mud in Boryeong contains healing properties so, as any self-respecting health fanatic knows, this means it's time to get all your friends together and get completely covered in the stuff from head to toe.

THIS SOUNDS LIKE FUN.

Millions of mud wrestlers can't be wrong, right? The mineral-rich mud attracts excitable local and international visitors all keen on getting completely slathered in the stuff. It's a family-friendly affair with activities that range from mud races and

slides, to the more sedate mud facials and body painting. There is even entertainment in the form of musical acts (hip hop and pop predominate) and spectacular evening fireworks. Don't leave before the Korean b-boy show on the Friday night.

AND IF WE DECIDE IT'S TIME TO CLEAN UP OUR ACT?

The festival puts on free showers so you can get the mud out of your eyes and ears (and the rest), but there's also the ocean nearby which is a welcome way to rinse off after a few hours in the sludge.

WWW.BUSOFEST.HU;

FEBRUARY.

Buso Festival, Mohács, Hungary

HUNGARIAN HALLOWEEN?

The creepy costumes donned by the revellers at this eccentric Magyar carnival certainly give Halloween ghouls a run for their money.

WHAT ARE THESE MASKED MEN DOING? AND WHY?

Dressed as horned monsters with woollen pelts, these costumed fiends are entrusted with the job of frightening off the freezing winter weather. It's a symbolic nod to a significant Hungarian historical event. In the 16th century, the townsfolk of Mohács dressed in disturbing get-up to frighten away the invading Turkish army.

ONCE THE AWFUL WEATHER HAS BEEN SENT PACKING, WHAT'S NEXT?

The festival lasts six days and over the course of this time there are lots of activities, open to all, that won't scare you silly. There's a costume competition for little monsters, a street procession that starts off on boats on the Danube and ends with horse-drawn floats in the centre of town, and a burning man effigy to signal the end of the cold. Everyone walks around drinking mulled wine and brandy and toasting their success at seeing in the imminent end of winter.

Dia de los Muertos, Mexico City, Mexico

DEATH ISN'T USUALLY A GOOD REASON FOR A RAUCOUS PARTY.

Try telling Mexico that. The widely observed and wildly popular 'Day of the Dead' festival is more about a joyous celebration of life than it is a subdued mourning of the dead.

HOW ON EARTH DID THIS COME ABOUT?

It's believed that the modern Mexican celebrations originated in indigenous traditions and rituals over 3000 years old. By the late 20th century the customs had developed to honour the deaths of children on 1 November and adults on 2 November.

WHAT ACTUALLY HAPPENS AT THESE DEATHLY PARTIES?

Families will decorate the graves of their lost loves as well as set up altars in their homes with the deceased's favourite food, drink, candles, flowers and incense in order to wish them well in the next world. The exuberant celebrations include dressing up in masks and painting faces. The ubiquitous skull motif has become a symbol of the festival, as it's designed to remind us that no matter what we are in life, we are the same in death.

WWW.STORICOCARNEVALEIVREA.IT;
FEBRUARY.

Ivrea Orange Festival, Ivrea, Turin, Italy

A FRUIT FESTIVAL SOUNDS VERY QUAINT.
That's what we thought, but no, this is war.

WAR DOESN'T SOUND LIKE MUCH FUN.
Ok, it's not exactly war, but a re-enactment of an historic battle between the victorious yet humble village folk and a despotic lord – instead of using more historically accurate weaponry like swords, the actors use oranges.

OF COURSE THEY DO. THAT MAKES PERFECT SENSE.
It's thought that the use of oranges came about after young women decided to drop oranges from balconies on high onto boys below that they found attractive... but ignoring the nonsensical sequence of events that got us here, the festival is a colourful, entertaining, vibrant spectacle watched by over 100,000 spectators. It's not possible for just anyone to take part in the actual battle, however; you need to register to be part of the regiment of foot soldiers.

OH GOOD, WE CAN STAND SAFELY ON THE SIDELINES AND CHEER THE VILLAGERS ON.
Sure, but be warned, being anywhere near the town square while the oranges are being launched will put you at risk of copping a juicing.

Kanamara Matsuri Festival, Kawasaki, Japan

THIS PRETTY MUCH TAKES THE CAKE.
If you thought Finland was out there with its wife-carrying and air guitar obsessions, then here comes the weirdness to outdo all weirdness.

IS THAT A...?
Yes ma'am, it sure is. The English translation of this festival's name is the Festival of the Iron Phallus. We're betting you haven't seen quite so many penises out in the open, in one place, at one time. The penis parade that happens in the afternoon on the day of the festival is a sight to behold; in particular, the phalluses put up on the pedestals are impressive in their anatomical correctness.

SEEMS A TOUCH GRATUITOUS.
For Westerners, the sight of so many model penises on display, some of which are the size of a standing human being, for example, can be confronting or amusing, depending on your point of view. However, the meaning behind the festival isn't so token or gratuitous – the point of the festival for many normally reserved Japanese is to celebrate fertility, marriage, birth and healthy sex.

WWW.LATOMATINA.INFO;

LAST WEDNESDAY IN AUGUST.

La Tomatina, Bunol, Valencia, Spain

THIS HAS GOT TO BE ONE OF THE MESSIEST FESTIVALS WE'VE EVER SEEN.

We'll give you a hot tip – don't wear your Sunday finest. You can expect to get entirely covered from tip to toe in squished tomatoes at this annual food fight festival in Eastern Spain.

AND THIS IS ALL IN AID OF WHAT?

A rollicking good time. Is there a better reason? The origins of the festival aren't clear, but that doesn't stop thousands upon thousands of revellers turning up on the last Wednesday in August to hurl tomatoes at one another.

DO WE BRING OUR OWN TOMATOES?

The festival has grown to such extraordinary size that the town trucks in tonnes of the red missiles and dumps them in the centre of town for the food fighters to get stuck into.

HOW LONG DOES THE CHAOS LAST?

Partying lasts all week, but the messy part of the affair lasts just a few hours, from 11am to around 2pm. Most of the action happens close to the town centre, but the streets fanning out from there are all caught up in the mix, so you can expect to get pelted wherever you are.

Thaipusam Festival, Batu Caves, Malaysia

ERM, WE MIGHT SIT THIS ONE OUT.

Deep breaths; this gnarly festival isn't a stickler for audience participation.

THAT'S A RELIEF. NOW WHAT ON EARTH IS GOING ON?

Thaipusam is observed around the world where there are significant Hindu Tamil populations. The celebrations centre around the remembrance of Lord Murugan, a Hindu god of war. He was apparently responsible for killing demons, thus demonstrating the triumph of good over evil.

SURE, BUT WHERE DOES THE WHOLE SKEWER THROUGH SKIN BIT COME IN?

The extreme flagellation is a way of showing atonement for sins and a commitment to overcoming temptations. The devotees carry their *kavadi* (burden) from Kuala Lumpur to the Batu Caves (approximately 9km) balanced on the piercings in their bodies. Once at the caves, they offer their burden to the gods and pledge their fidelity to family and divinities. It's a custom passed down from generation to generation, and despite the somewhat gruesome nature of the event, you'll see all members of the family getting involved, all the way from children to grandparents.

WWW.UFOFESTIVALROSWELL.COM;

LATE JUNE TO EARLY JULY.

UFO Festival, Roswell, New Mexico, USA

SO THE TRUTH IS OUT THERE!

If truckloads of alien paraphernalia and tens of thousands of alien-existence believers are anything to go by, then yes. The belief that there is something out there is alive and well at the world's premier UFO festival.

ROSWELL IS WHERE IT ALL HAPPENED, RIGHT?

Sure is – this is where the extra-terrestrial spaceship (aka military surveillance balloon) crash-landed in 1947. Don't feel left out if you're a believer in the balloon over the spaceship;

the festival actively welcomes any sceptics out there who might need some convincing.

WITH A SHORTAGE OF ACTUAL ALIENS AND UFOS, WHAT ELSE HAS THE FESTIVAL GOT IN STORE?

Over the course of four days there are costume competitions, including one for your pet, if they enjoy getting their alien on too; an alien street parade; live musical entertainment; and guest speaking panels packed with authors who have been published on the topic of the moment – ETs and UFOs.

WWW.EUKONKANTO.FI;

JULY.

Wife Carrying Festival, Sonkajarvi, Finland

EXCUSE ME? THERE'S A FESTIVAL WHERE YOU CARRY YOUR WIFE AROUND THE WHOLE TIME?

Think of it more like the Olympics, than say, Lollapalooza. Teams of two, man and woman (not necessarily married, despite the name of the competition), go up against other teams to complete an obstacle course in the fastest time possible, with the woman held aloft by the man for the entire time.

THAT ALL SOUNDS TOTALLY NORMAL.

Finland is one for weird and wacky festivals – see the Air Guitar World Championship (page 102). But before you go

thinking that this is all fun and games, we'll have you know that this wife carrying business is serious. Teams put in months of training for the event, and over many years different holds have been developed in order to quicken the pace – the hold of the moment is known as 'the Estonian', where the wife is upside down with her legs around her 'husband's' neck.

WE HOPE THE WINNERS ARE RICHLY REWARDED.

Indeed they are. In another example of Finnish originality, the victorious duo is awarded the 'wife's' weight in beer.

About the author

Kalya Ryan loves a good party, so when she sees the opportunity to mix travel with festivities, good luck holding her back. Music is her favourite reason for group merrymaking, but she wouldn't mind witnessing some of the weirder get-togethers, like Scotland's Up Helly Aa Fire Festival, before she runs out of steam.

Index

North America

Oceania

South America

More things to blow your mind

50 Bars to Blow Your Mind

Lonely Planet handpicks the world's most extraordinary drinking holes, from caverns and island party havens to a bar nestled in an ancient tree trunk.
ISBN 978-1-76034-058-2

50 Museums to Blow Your Mind

Whether you're a history buff, tech-head or have an inexplicable fascination with clowns, you'll find world-class collections here to pique your interest.
ISBN 978-1-76034-060-5

50 Beaches to Blow Your Mind

Discover the planet's most pristine, jaw-dropping, wild and wonderful sandy spots.

ISBN 978-1-76034-059-9

50 Natural Wonders to Blow Your Mind

A tour of the world's most wild and wonderful places: discover just how extraordinary our planet really is.
ISBN 978-1-78657-406-0

50 Places to Stay to Blow Your Mind

With these extraordinary offerings around the world, even sleeping will be an adventure on your next trip.
ISBN 978-1-78657-405-3

Published in May 2017 by Lonely Planet Global Limited, CRN 554153
www.lonelyplanet.com
ISBN 978 1 78657 404 6
© Lonely Planet 2017
Printed in China
10 9 8 7 6 5 4 3 2 1

Written by **Kalya Ryan**
Managing Director, Publishing **Piers Pickard**
Associate Publisher **Robin Barton**
Commissioning Editor **Jessica Cole**
Art Direction **Daniel Di Paolo**
Layout Designer **Austin Taylor**
Editor **Kate Turvey**
Picture Researcher **Christina Webb**
Print Production **Larissa Frost, Nigel Longuet**
Cover image Holi Festival, India © **Poras Chaudhary**

Lonely Planet offices

STAY IN TOUCH lonelyplanet.com/contact

AUSTRALIA The Malt Store, Level 3, 551 Swanston St, Carlton, Victoria 3053
03 8379 8000

IRELAND Unit E, Digital Court, The Digital Hub, Rainsford St, Dublin 8

USA 124 Linden St, Oakland, CA 94607,
510 250 6400

UNITED KINGDOM 240 Blackfriars Rd, London SE1 8NW, 020 3771 5100